CITY

CITY

A Story of Roman Planning and Construction

DAVID MACAULAY

Clarion Books
An Imprint of HarperCollins*Publishers*
Boston   New York

For Janice
and things to come

special thanks to Hardu, Mary,
Sidney, Bill, my parents,
Melanie, Walter and Vitruvius.

Library of Congress Cataloging in Publication Data

Macaulay, David.
   City; a story of Roman planning and construction.

   SUMMARY: Text and black and white illustrations
show how the Romans planned and constructed their cities
for the people who lived within them.
   1. Civil engineering — Rome (City) — Juvenile literature.   2. Rome (City) — Antiquities — Juvenile literature.
3. Building — Rome (City) — Juvenile literature.
4. Cities and towns — Planning — Rome (City) — Juvenile
literature.   [1. Civil engineering — Rome (City)
2. Rome (City) — Antiquities.   3. Building — Rome (City)]
I. Title.
TA80.R6M3   711'.4'0937   74-4280

ISBN: 978-0-395-19492-8 (CI)
ISBN: 978-0-395-34922-9 (Pa)

Printed in Vietnam

23 SCP 45 44 43 42 41

By 200 B.C. soldiers of the Roman Republic had conquered all of Italy except the Alps. In the following three hundred years they created an empire extending from Spain to the Persian Gulf. To insure their hold over these lands the Roman soldiers built permanent military camps. As the need for military force lessened, many camps became important cities of the Roman Empire. The Romans knew that well planned cities did more to maintain peace and security than twice the number of military camps. They also knew that a city was more than just a business, government, or religious center. It was all three, but most important, it had to be a place where people wanted to live.

Because cities were built either where no city previously existed or where a small village stood, the maximum population and size were determined before construction began. The planners then allotted adequate space for houses, shops, squares, and temples. They decided how much water would be needed and the number and size of streets, sidewalks, and sewers. By planning this way they tried to satisfy the needs of every individual — rich and poor alike.

The planners agreed that when a city reached its maximum population a new city should be built elsewhere. They recognized the danger of overpopulation. A city forced to grow beyond its walls not only burdened the existing water, sewage, and traffic systems but eventually destroyed the farmland on whose crops the people depended.

Although Verbonia is imaginary, its planning and construction are based on those of the hundreds of Roman cities founded between 300 B.C. and A.D. 150. No matter what brought about their creation, they were designed and built to serve the needs of all the people who lived within them. This kind of planning is the basis of any truly successful city. The need for it today is greater than ever.

For almost two hundred years the wheat and grapes of northern Italy's fertile Po Valley had been collected in small trading villages and shipped to Rome. In 26 B.C. a disastrous spring flood destroyed the villages along the Po riverbanks as well as an important bridge. When news reached the Emperor Augustus he immediately dispatched to the stricken area forty-five military engineers, including planners, architects, surveyors, and construction specialists. They were to supervise the building of a new bridge and new roads and to lay plans for a new city. The city was named Verbonia, and — in honor of the Emperor — Augusta Verbonia.

Augustus hoped to combine all the remaining trading villages into one secure and efficient trading center and so increase the amount of produce coming into Rome. To speed up development of the new city, he retired to the area two thousand soldiers, who would not only help build Verbonia but also become its first citizens.

First the surveyors selected the place where the city would be built. They chose a flat but sloping site (to insure good drainage) that was high enough to avoid future floods. A Roman priest examined the livers of a rabbit and a pheasant from the area to find out if it would be a healthy place in which to live. When the animals were found to be without fault and an investigation of the land turned up no stagnant pools, the gods were thanked and the choice of the site was officially confirmed.

The soldiers and the slaves who traveled with them then set up a military camp called a castrum. First they dug a protective ditch and erected a stockade fence around a rectangular area. Next the two main streets were marked off — one running from north to south, the other from east to west. They crossed at right angles above a long open space called the forum where the soldiers would gather daily to receive their orders. At one end of the forum the

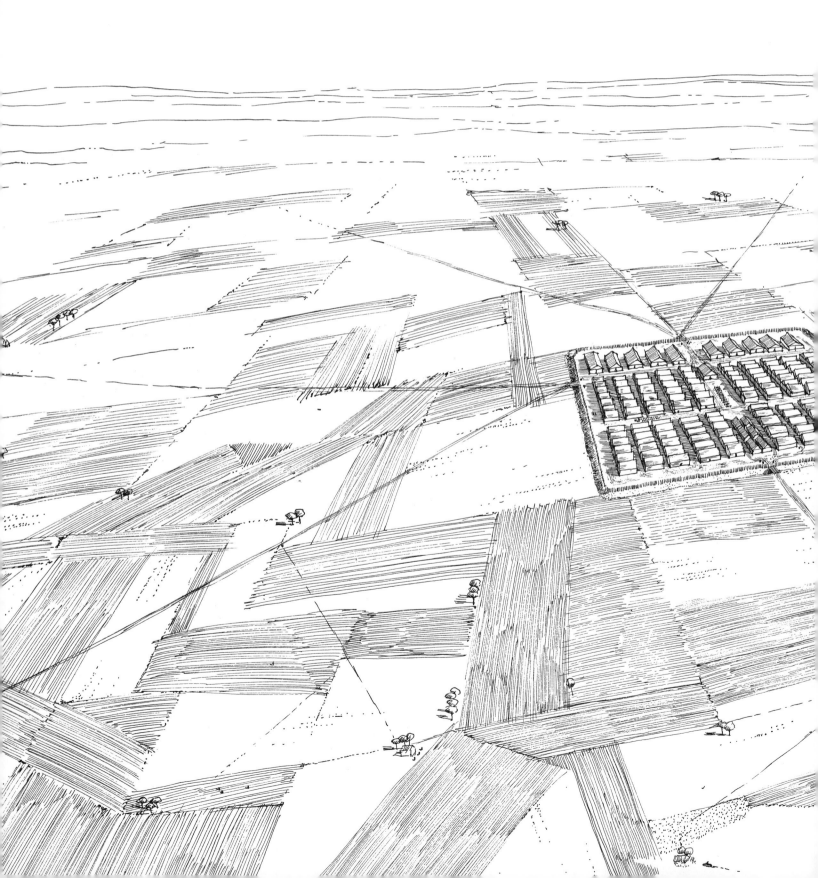

commander's tent was pitched. The tents for soldiers, slaves, and supplies filled the remainder of the castrum and were grouped in rows. In the following months all the tents were replaced by more permanent wooden shelters and a temporary bridge was constructed over boats anchored side by side across the river.

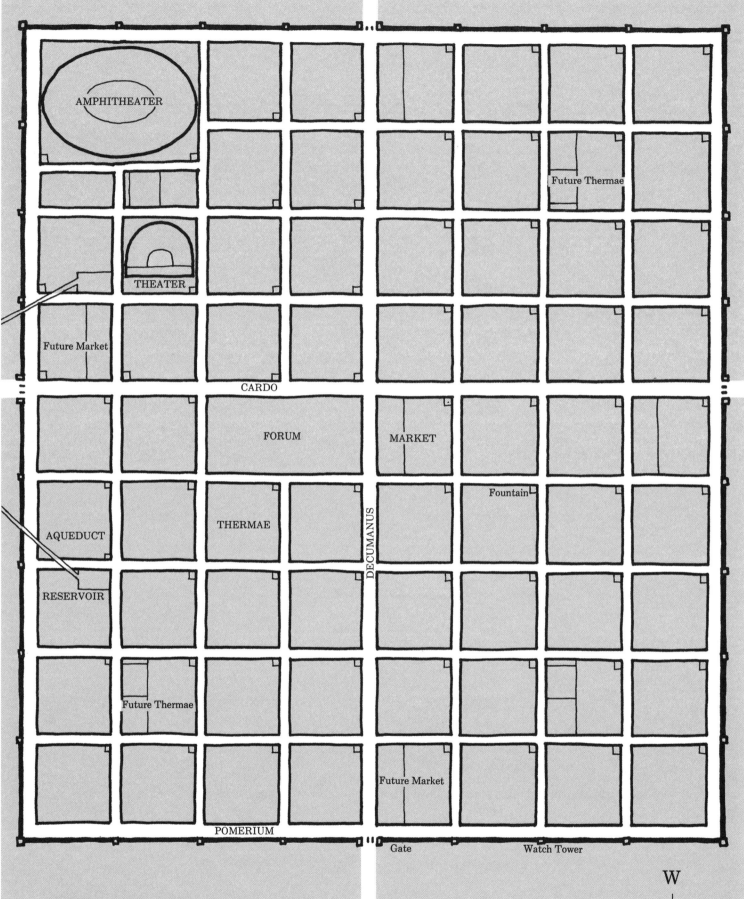

AMPHITHEATER

Future Thermae

THEATER

Future Market

CARDO

FORUM

MARKET

Fountain

AQUEDUCT

THERMAE

DECUMANUS

RESERVOIR

Future Thermae

POMERIUM

Future Market

Gate

Watch Tower

VERBONIA
THE MASTER PLAN

W

S —|— N

E

The engineers worked throughout the winter measuring, designing, and drawing. By the spring of 25 B.C. (the Roman year 728) the master plan for Verbonia was ready. The center of the castrum became the center of the city. The main street running from north to south was now called the cardo, the one from east to west, the decumanus. Both were widened and lengthened and the rectangular area of the camp was increased to seven hundred and twenty yards long by six hundred and twenty yards wide. This space allowed a maximum population of approximately 50,000. A greater number, the planners believed, would make the city too large and unable to meet the needs of the people.

The entire area was divided by roads into a chessboard pattern. Almost all of the blocks, called insulae, were eighty yards square. A high wall was designed around the city in which fortified gates were located where the main streets cut through. Around the city but inside the wall a thirty-foot-wide strip of land called the pomerium was marked off. It represented the sacred boundary of the city within which the land was protected by the gods.

The city planners indicated those facilities which served all the residents. They designed a new and larger forum which was to become the government and religious center of the city. They located public water fountains, the aqueduct that would bring the water, a central food market, public baths and toilets, and an entertainment center made up of a theater and amphitheater. They also set aside spaces for future buildings.

No privately owned building, they decreed, could be higher than twice the width of the street on which it stood. This insured that sunlight always reached the streets. They also required all persons whose buildings faced one of the main streets to build, at their own expense, shelter over the sidewalk for the comfort and protection of all pedestrians.

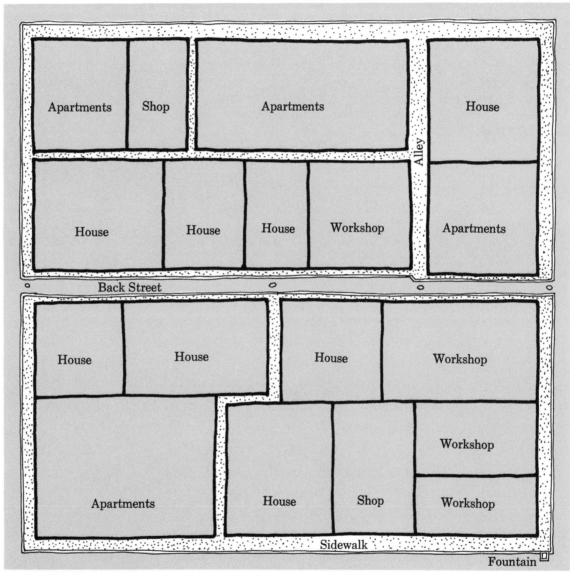

TYPICAL INSULA

The master plan allowed much freedom for the residents to determine the appearance and character of the city through the buildings they would construct for themselves. Each insula, left deliberately empty on the plan, would eventually be filled with buildings of all sizes and be crossed by narrow back roads and alleys.

AVGVSTA VERBONIA
· DCCXXVIII ·

Some of the insulae designated for private ownership were divided up among the soldiers, traders, and farmers. The names of the owners and the sizes of their holdings were inscribed on the plan and sent to the land office in Rome. A copy of the plan was carved on marble and stood in the forum for everyone to see. Even though land was given to Verbonia's first settlers, each person had to pay for the construction of his own house.

In the early summer of 25 B.C. a plow drawn by a white cow and a white bull guided by a Roman priest cut a furrow around the site. This solemn religious ceremony marked the location of the city wall and insured further protection by the gods. The plow was lifted only where gates were to be built.

Following the ceremony the surveyors marked off the roads using an instrument called a groma to make certain that all roads intersected at right angles. The groma was a pole about four feet high on top of which a cross was laid flat. When weighted strings hanging from each end of the cross hung parallel to the center pole the groma was known to be perpendicular to the ground. The streets could be accurately marked off by sighting down the intersecting arms of the cross.

The same method was used to mark off roads and farmland outside the city.

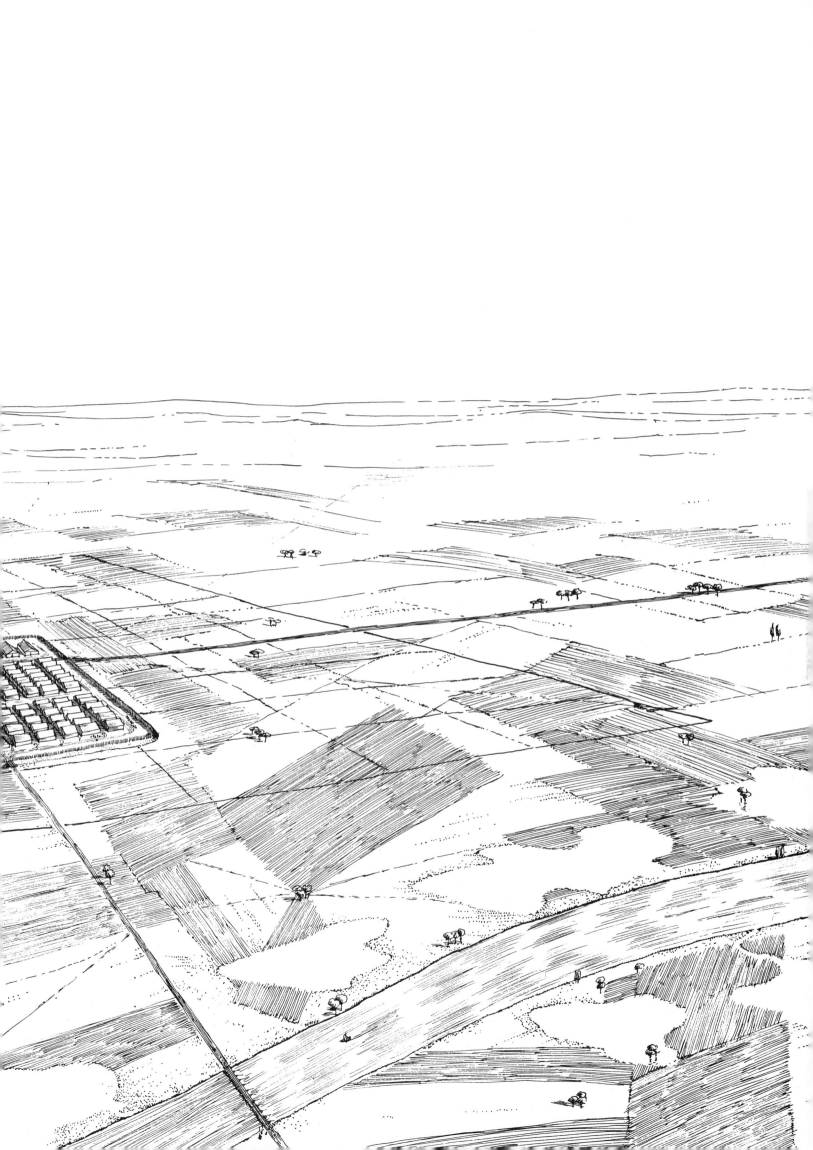

The materials used most in the construction of Verbonia were stone, clay, mortar, and wood. The stone came from a limestone quarry owned by the government. Besides many work sheds, the quarry contained a forge for making and repairing tools and a carpenter's shop in which cranes and pulleys were built.

The skilled laborers cut, polished, or carved inscriptions in the stone. The unskilled workers separated and lifted the huge blocks from the earth. The stone was usually cut with a saw. When the stone was very hard, the blade used in the saw had no teeth; sand and steel filings were placed under the blade and the back-and-forth motion of the saw ground away the stone.

When the stone could not be sawed, a row of holes was drilled where it was to be divided. Wooden stakes were then jammed into the holes. When water was poured over the stakes, they swelled, splitting the stone along the line of holes.

The clay was made into bricks and tiles in factories near Arretium. The clay, dug out of large pits in the ground, was formed into standard shapes and sizes using wooden molds. The mold was then removed and the wet clay placed in an oven to dry and harden. All bricks and tiles were stamped with the name of the factory owner and the name of the Emperor.

The mortar used between bricks and stones and in concrete was a mixture of sand, lime (a powder obtained by burning limestone), and water. When mortar was used in construction underwater, a gravelly substance called pozzolana was added which made the mortar become extremely hard whcn it set.

The wood used for scaffolding and roof framework came from a forest at the foot of the Apennine mountains to the south.

Before building could begin, laborers had to be found. Besides the soldiers many poor farmers from the countryside came to work and settle in the city. The majority of workers however were slaves, either owned by the state or by wealthy businessmen, or they were prisoners of war from Gaul, Greece, or Egypt. Unless they were skilled, the laborers were formed into work gangs to do jobs requiring no particular skill. To maintain as high a level of work as possible the laborers were treated almost as well as the soldiers.

Saw

Compass

Pattern

Hammer

Measuring Stick

Chisel

Pattern

Pickax

Square

Drill

STONEWORKING TOOLS

Ax

Auger

Sledge Hammer

Wedge

Spansaw

Ax

Plane

Pincers

A great variety of tools was needed throughout the construction of the city. Most were made in forges and workshops on the site. The more precise measuring instruments and squares were brought from Rome.

The new roads and bridge were completed before work began on the city itself. Once the surveyors had marked out a road with stakes, a ditch was dug on each side into which a row of curbstones was set. A deeper ditch was then dug between the two rows of curbstones which was filled with layers of stones of varying size. The top layer formed the pavement of the road and rose slightly in the center to force the rainwater into the side ditches. The pavement was constructed of flat stones that were carefully fitted together. Any spaces left between them were filled with smaller stones or pieces of scrap iron.

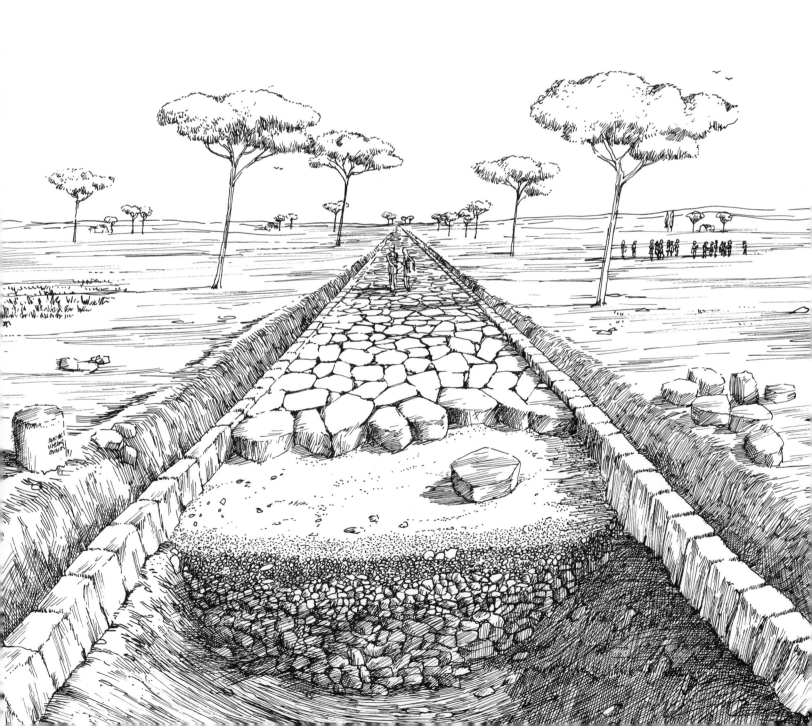

From the boat bridge work began on the permanent bridge. It was to be made of wood and supported on five stone towers called piers which were to stand in the river. Cofferdams were built so the laborers could erect the piers without having to work underwater. First, piles were driven into the riverbed. These were oak tree trunks, with all the bark scraped off, chiseled to a point at the bottom. They were chained together vertically in a shape around which the river could easily flow. When the gaps between the piles had been filled with clay, the water was pumped out of the enclosed area.

Each pier stood on a foundation of tar-covered piles and was constructed of carefully cut stones on the outside and smaller uncut stones on the inside. The mortar used between the stones contained pozzolana. When the piers reached a height of thirty feet above the river, wooden arches were hoisted into place between them.

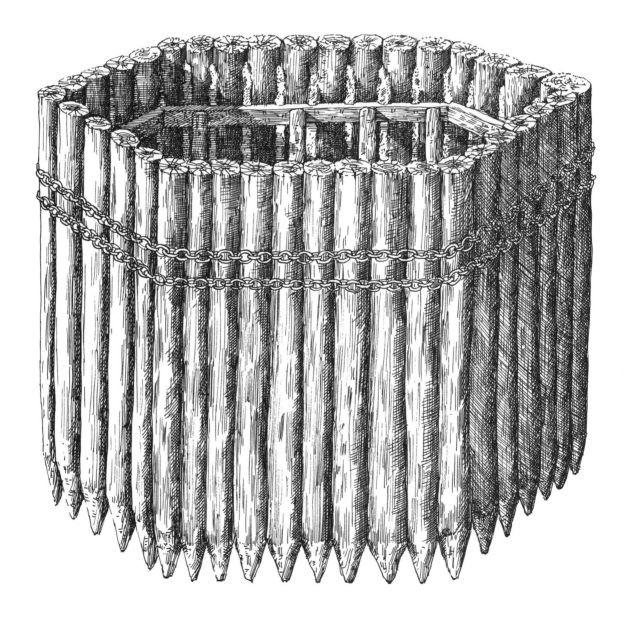

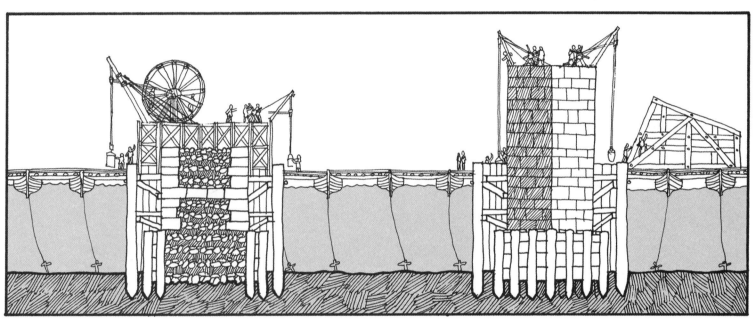

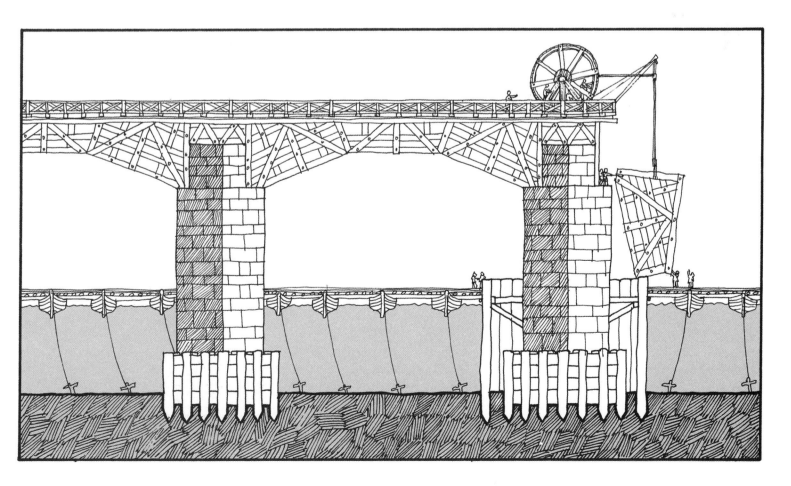

A wooden road was nailed to the arches and covered with a layer of earth.
The finished road stood almost sixty feet above the river.

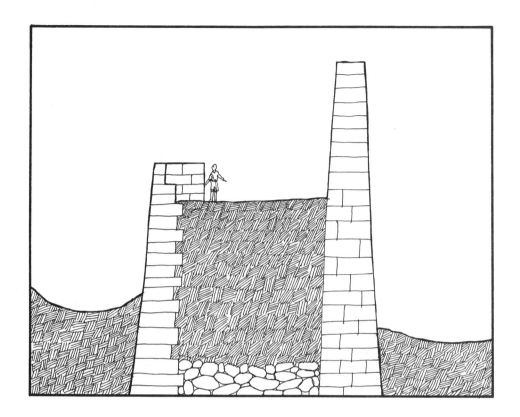

The city wall was built next. Two large ditches were dug along the furrow and the dirt was heaped into a high mound between them. A stone wall was built against each side for additional strength. The base of the outer wall went down thirty feet below ground level, making it almost impossible for anyone to tunnel under. On top of the outer wall alternating high and low sections called crenelations were built. The soldiers were protected behind the high sections while firing their weapons over the low sections. The inner wall was several feet higher than the outer wall to block the path of rocks and arrows that might be fired into the city.

Cranes on top of the mound lowered the stones into place. Four men standing inside a wooden wheel at the base of the crane provided the power. As they walked forward the wheel turned, rotating an axle which wound the rope. The engineers constantly checked to make sure each course of stones was level.

Each gate contained three vaulted openings, one for the road and another for each sidewalk. When the walls on both sides of the road were finished, a wooden arch called a centering was supported between them on projecting stones. The masons, working from both sides, then placed wedge-shaped stones on top of the centering. When the keystone was inserted in the center, the arch was complete. The centering was then moved sideways and another arch was constructed next to the first. This process was repeated until the entire passageway was covered by a semicircular roof called a tunnel vault. The sidewalks were covered in the same way.

The openings in the gate were sealed by heavy wooden doors. The central opening was also protected by a wooden grate called a portcullis, lowered from a room above the street. Both the doors and the portcullis were covered with bronze plates.

Along the wall and on each side of the main gates high watchtowers were built for additional protection.

At first, Verbonia's drinking water came from several deep wells within the city walls. But the planners knew that as the population increased the wells would no longer be sufficient. A pipeline called an aqueduct was proposed to bring water from the mountain lakes thirty-eight miles to the south.

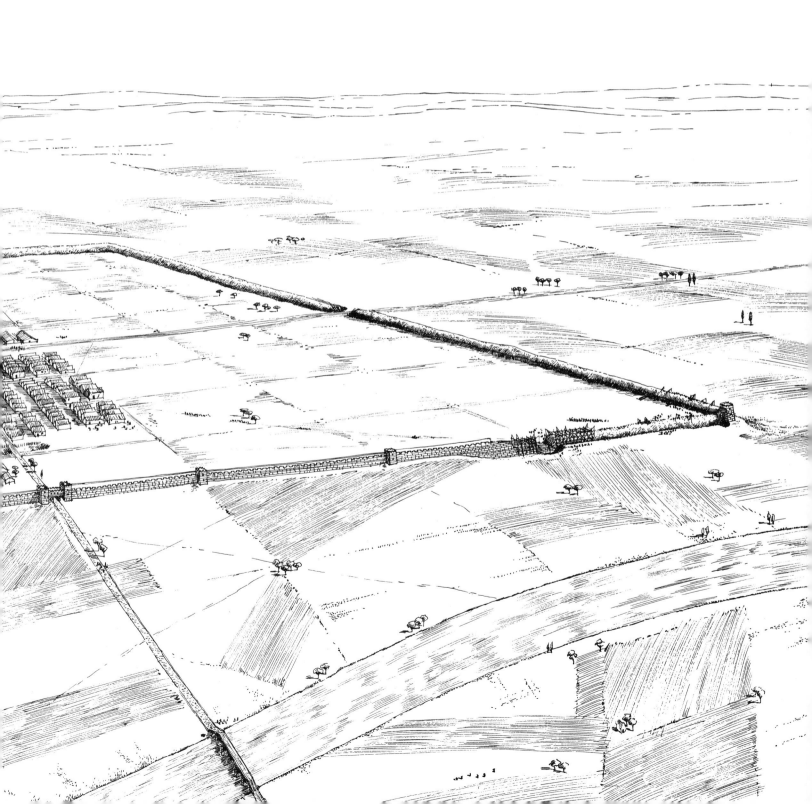

When the best route for the aqueduct had been chosen, a profile map of the land was drawn showing the hills and valleys. To determine the profile, surveyors used leveling instruments called chorobates. The chorobate was known to be level when weighted strings fastened to the horizontal bar hung parallel to the legs. This was double-checked by pouring water into a groove on top of the horizontal bar. When the distance between the top of the water and the top of the bar was the same all around the groove, the instrument was level.

By sighting along the chorobate the surveyors were able to create an imaginary horizontal line over the entire route of the aqueduct. Every forty feet along this line the vertical distance between it and the ground was recorded. When the line was drawn on parchment the vertical distances were marked below it. By connecting all the marks with a single line the mapmakers obtained an accurate profile of the land. By then drawing the line of the aqueduct on the plan the engineers could easily see whether it would sit on the ground, cut through the ground, or rise above the ground.

The aqueduct had to be built with a constant slope from beginning to end to keep the water moving.

To prevent people from stealing or poisoning the water, most of the aqueduct was raised about fifty feet off the ground. It was supported by a continuous row of arches built on tall square piers which rested on deep foundations.

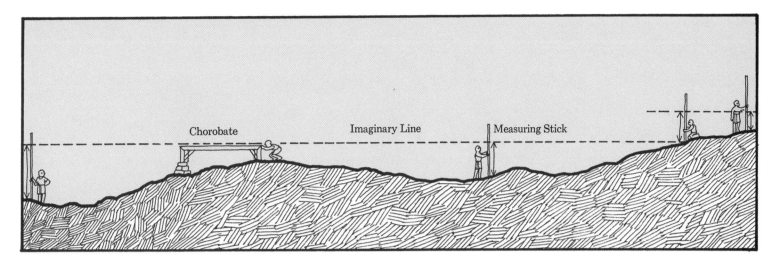

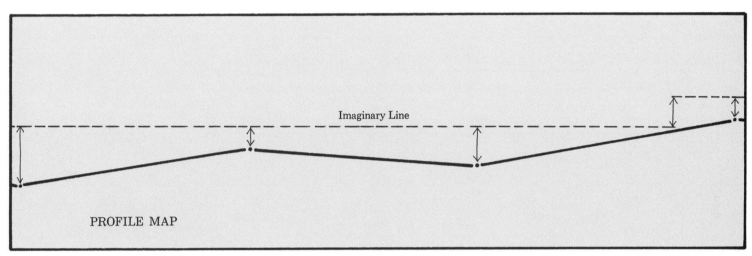

PROFILE MAP

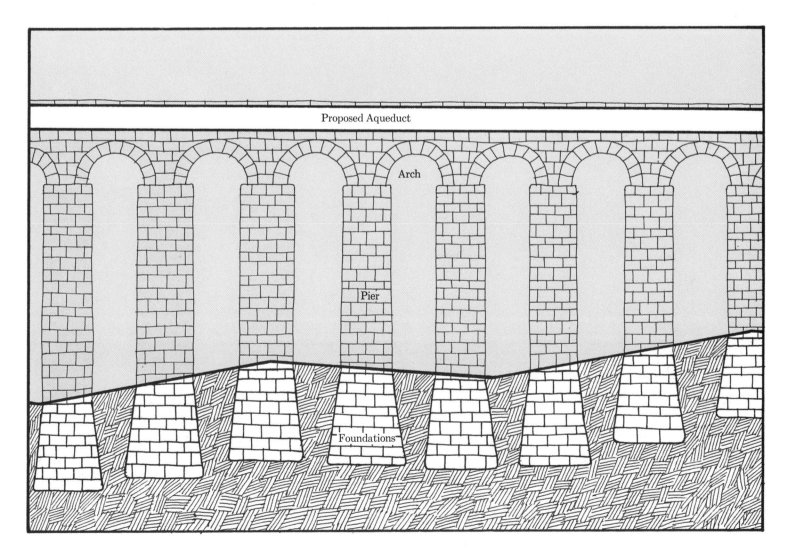

The foundations and piers were constructed of stone-faced concrete — stone set in mortar on the outside with layers of concrete on the inside. To make the concrete, the masons first laid a course of rough stones across the area to be filled. The mortar men then covered the stones with a layer of mortar to bind them together. When the mortar had set, the process was repeated.

When two piers were finished, an arch was constructed between them. The aqueduct, itself a rectangular stone pipe about four feet wide and six feet high, was then built on top. The inner surface of the pipe was lined with hard cement to prevent leaks.

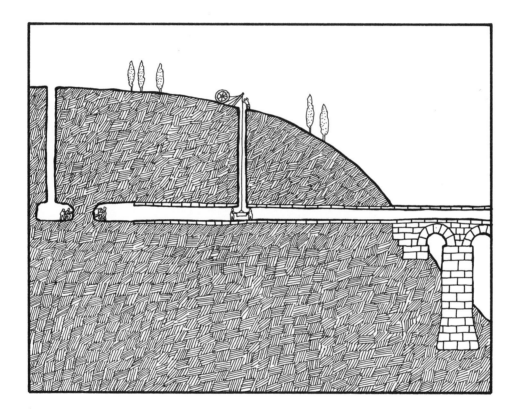

The route chosen for the aqueduct required that a short tunnel be dug through a hill. Every twenty yards vertical shafts were sunk from the surface of the hill to the level of the proposed aqueduct. The depths of the shafts were measured from the profile plan.

The laborers connected the ends of the shafts, and as a section was completed the masons lined it with stone and cement.

Appius Fluvius, the chief water engineer, rode out from the city once a week to inspect construction. The foremen and laborers lived in camp sites which moved with the aqueduct farther and farther from the city. For twenty miles the aqueduct ran alongside the main highway, and the laborers would often stop

to watch the endless procession of merchants and farmers. About three years after construction began, large numbers of families could be seen traveling toward the city. Many belonged to the soldiers stationed in Verbonia. During the fifth year of construction the aqueduct turned away from the highway and two years later it was completed.

Before the wall of the city was finished, work began on the streets. Verbonia's streets were designed for people. Therefore adequate sidewalks were built and strict laws were written to control any movement of carts and chariots which could endanger the health and safety of people in the streets.

During the day all carts and chariots except those carrying building materials were banned from the streets. This meant that deliveries had to be made at night or in the early morning. Carts and horses were very noisy, so many of the streets on which people lived were made one way or dead end to reduce traffic.

The sidewalks on both sides of the streets were raised one and a half feet above the road surface. This precaution prevented vehicles from accidentally rolling into the path of pedestrians. Steppingstones were embedded in the middle of the road to connect the sidewalks. Animals and carts could straddle the stones — but only if they went slowly. In this way the stones helped to enforce the speed limit. When it rained, the streets were the gutters through which water ran into sewers under the sidewalks. The steppingstones enabled people to cross the street without getting their sandals drenched. The cardo and decumanus were finished first. Other streets were completed as the area around them developed.

In 20 B.C. Appius and his staff started on the supply system that would distribute water throughout the city. The aqueduct was carried over the south wall and connected to two reservoirs. These were deep rectangular pools whose walls were brick-faced concrete — a wall of triangular bricks on the inside and outside enclosing layers of concrete. Every few feet the top of the wall was covered with three courses of large flat bricks. This allowed the contractor to adjust the level of the wall if it was not perfect.

Each reservoir was covered by a concrete tunnel vault. The vaults were constructed over a semicircular wooden form supported on scaffolding between the sides of the pool. Brick reinforcing arches were first constructed over the form ten feet apart. The entire form was then lined with flat bricks and covered with a thick layer of concrete. When the concrete hardened and could stand by itself the form was moved into the next position. Using the same form over and over, the process was repeated until the reservoir was covered. The brick facing on the inside surface of the vault and walls was covered with hard cement. The outside of the vault was shaped like a pitched roof and covered with tiles.

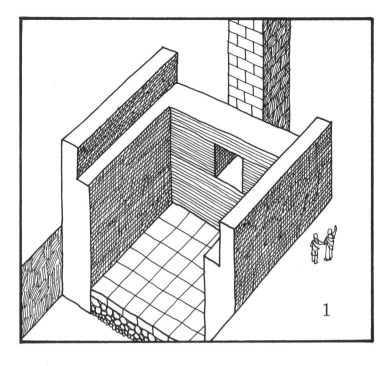 

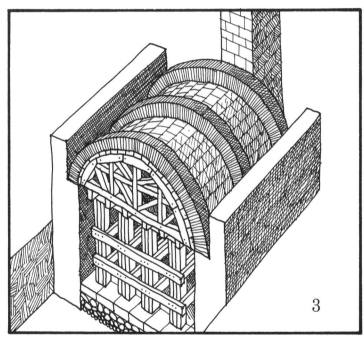 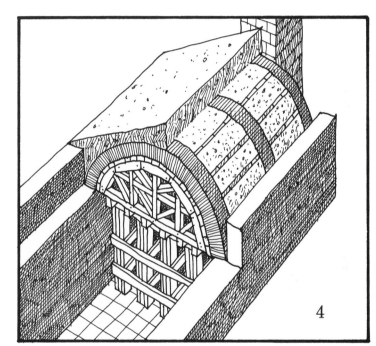

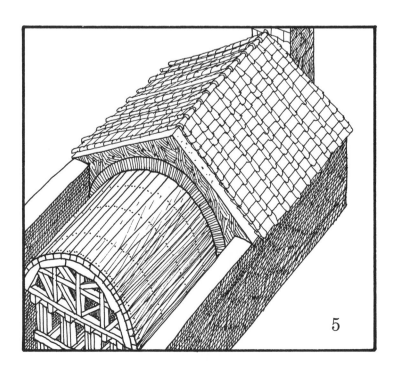 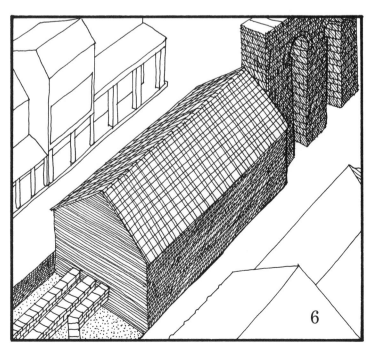

On the wall at one end of the reservoir were several gates channeling the water into lead pipes which ran either to public fountains, toilets, and baths, or to the homes of the wealthy. When there was a shortage of water, the gate leading to these homes was closed, and then, if necessary, the gate to the baths and toilets was closed as well. This insured that the public fountains supplying the majority of Verbonia's residents would be the last to run dry. The water for wealthy homes was first piped into a lead tank placed on one of many high brick towers. As it ran back down other pipes, the water gained enough pressure to feed all the houses to which the tower was connected.

In order for the water supply system to be efficient, an equally efficient drainage system was required. Sewers originally constructed under the sidewalks for rainwater were enlarged. They were connected to both public and private buildings by clay pipes. Some of the sewers were six feet deep. They were all built of stone and mortar and their tops were removable stone slabs in case repairs were necessary. The slabs were covered by compressed dirt in which the lead supply pipes from the water towers were laid.

All the sewers were connected to two cloacae — tunnels large enough to walk in — which carried the water under the walls of the city and down to the river. Iron grills were installed inside them which let the water out but prevented anyone from getting in.

By 19 B.C. the city walls were finished and work began on the first and most important public areas of the city — the forum and the market.

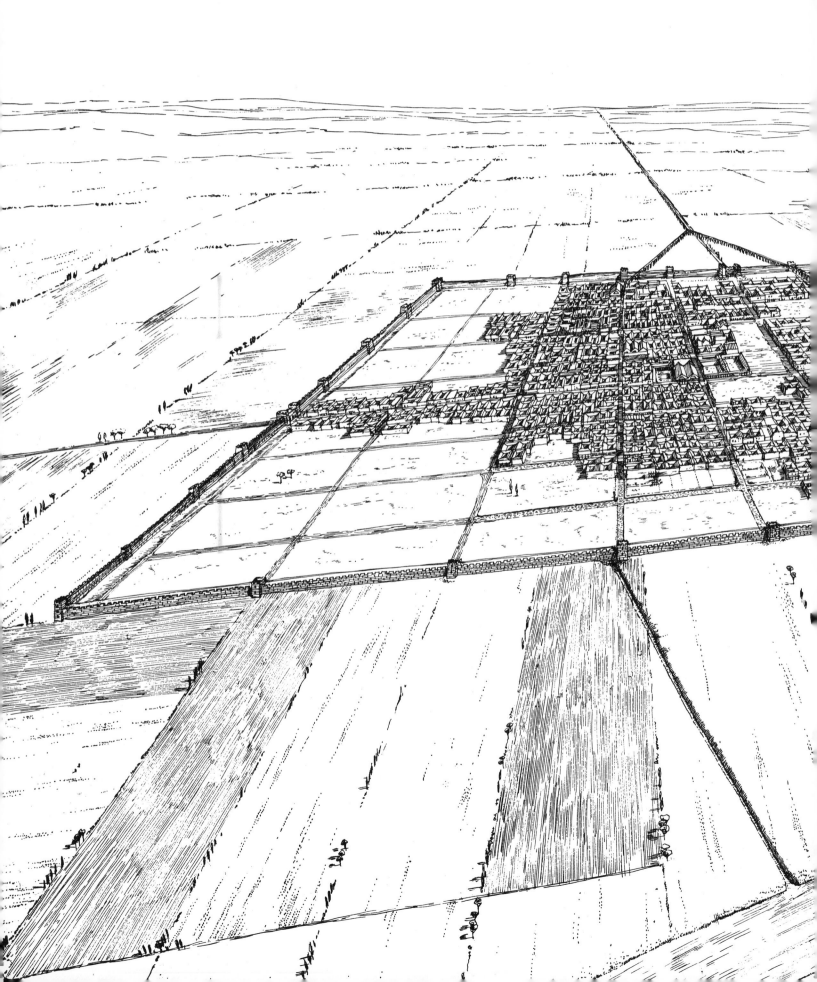

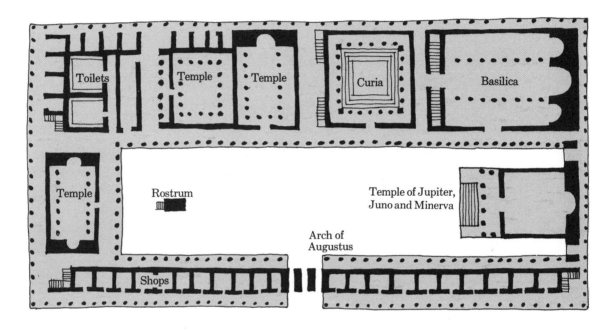

THE FORUM · PLAN

The forum was paved and covered two entire blocks. At one end the temple of Jupiter, Juno, and Minerva was built. Of all the temples to be built in the forum this was the most important. At the opposite end, facing the temple, was the rostrum. This was a raised platform from which speeches were made and decrees were read to the residents of the city. Along one side of the forum stood the Curia — the building in which the elected senators of the city met. Next to the Curia was the Basilica, the court of justice. The temple was constructed of polished limestone, while the other two buildings were brick-faced concrete covered with sheets of limestone. All the roofs were made of triangular wooden frames called trusses, covered by rows of clay tiles.

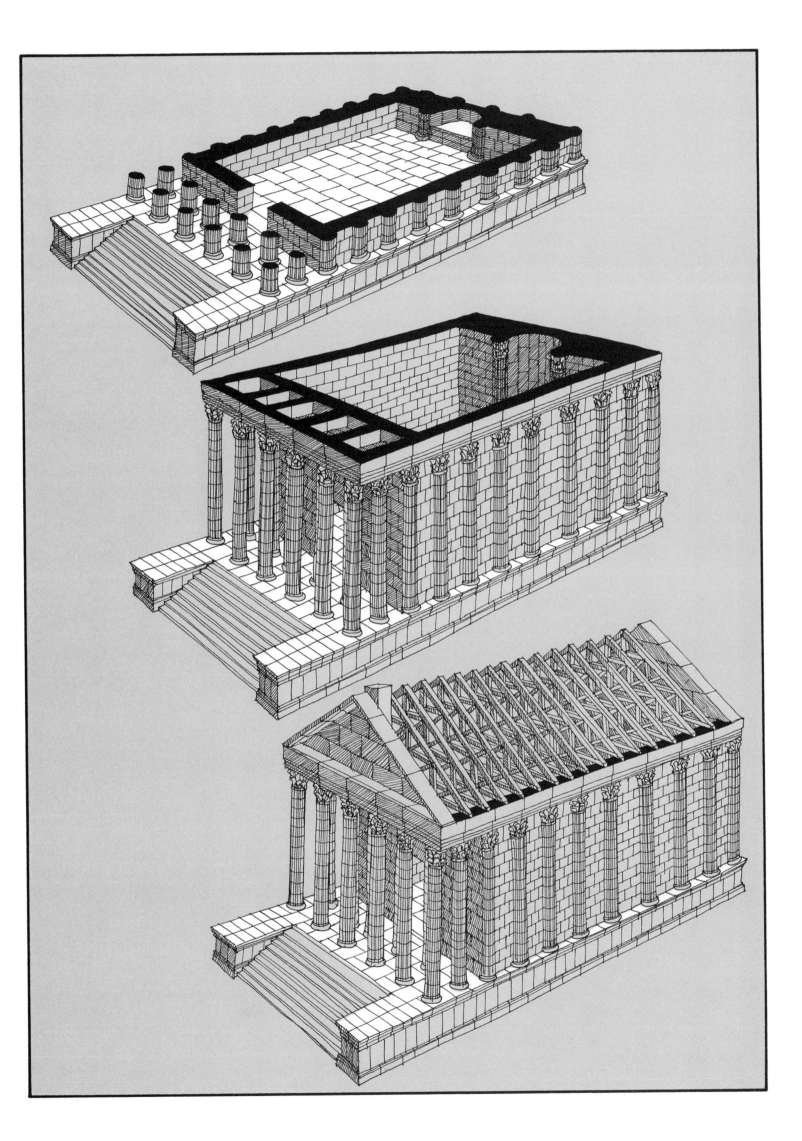

The buildings and the forum were surrounded by rows of columns called colonnades. The columns were either built of cylindrical stone blocks set on top of each other or they were constructed of brick and mortar covered by cement.

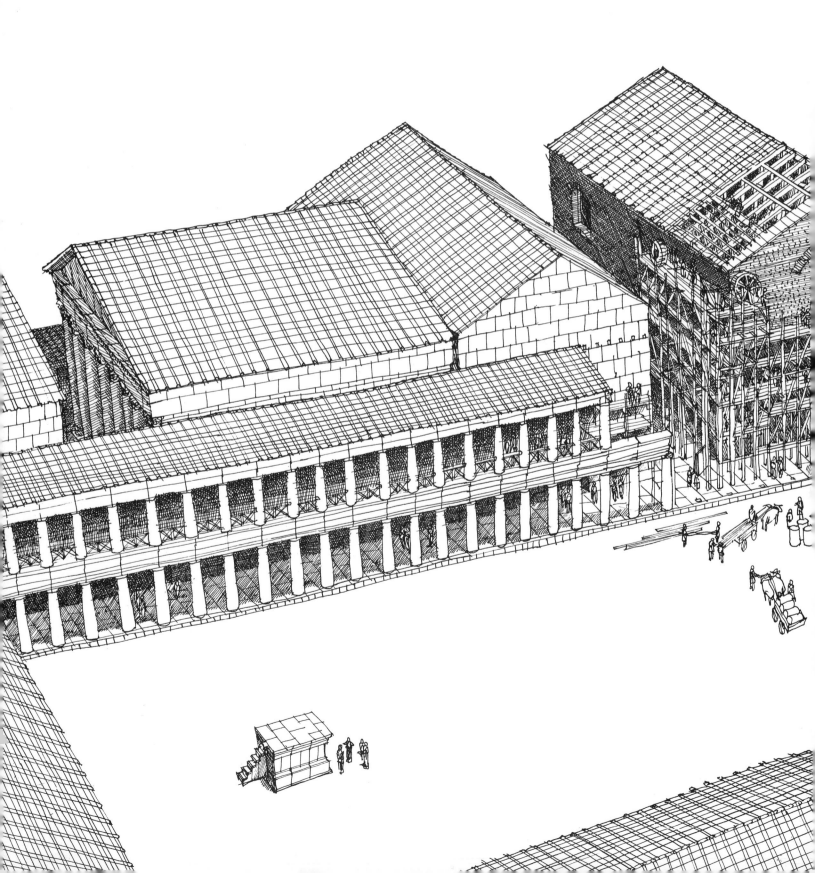

A long two-story structure enclosed on both sides by colonnades was built to separate the forum from the busy streets. On the lower level were little shops which faced the street. On the second level were offices and schoolrooms which faced the forum.

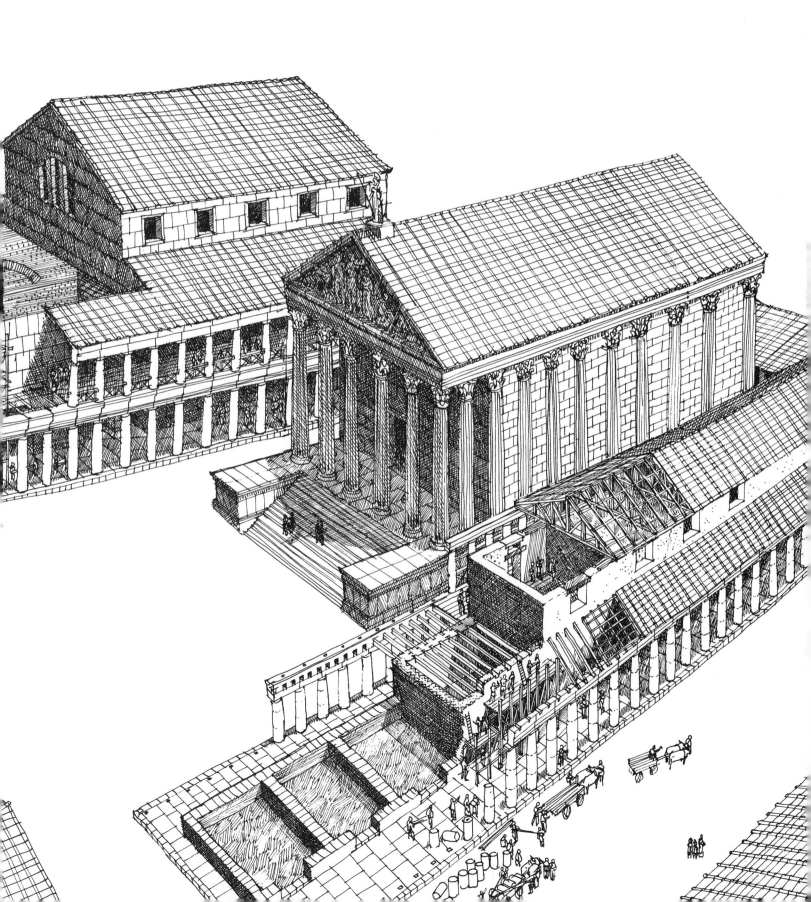

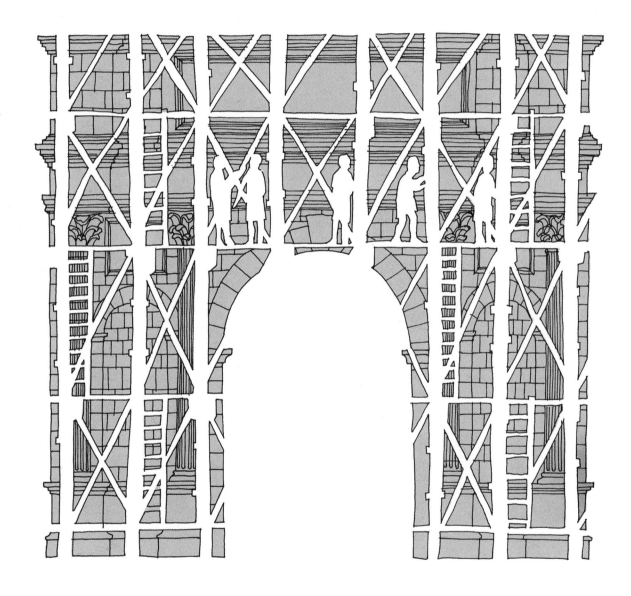

Over the main entrance to the forum, off the cardo, a large triumphal arch was constructed to the glory of the Emperor. It was made of brick-faced concrete and covered with sheets of colored marble. On special holidays processions would enter the forum through the arch.

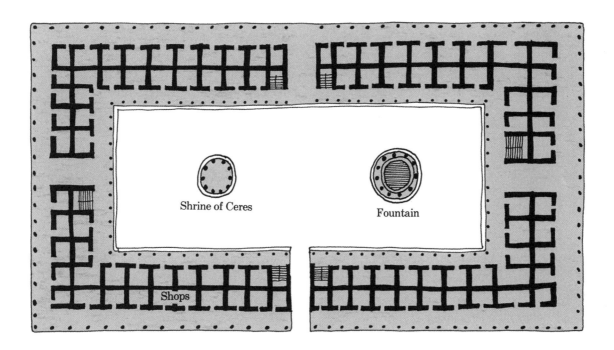

THE CENTRAL MARKET · PLAN

Because new temples were always being enlarged or replaced the forum really wasn't finished for two hundred years. But the central market across the street was finished in less than five. This was not surprising since Verbonia's main function was that of a trading center.

The open area in which farmers and merchants set up their stands covered almost half a block and was surrounded on all four sides by colonnades similar to those of the forum. In the center was a public fountain and a shrine to Ceres, the goddess of agriculture.

Many of the offices on the second level were rented by businessmen who kept similar offices in other cities, including Rome. These men bought much of the produce from the fields around the city and shipped it to markets all over the empire.

As open land within the walls gradually disappeared, the importance of careful planning became more and more evident — especially in two well-thought-

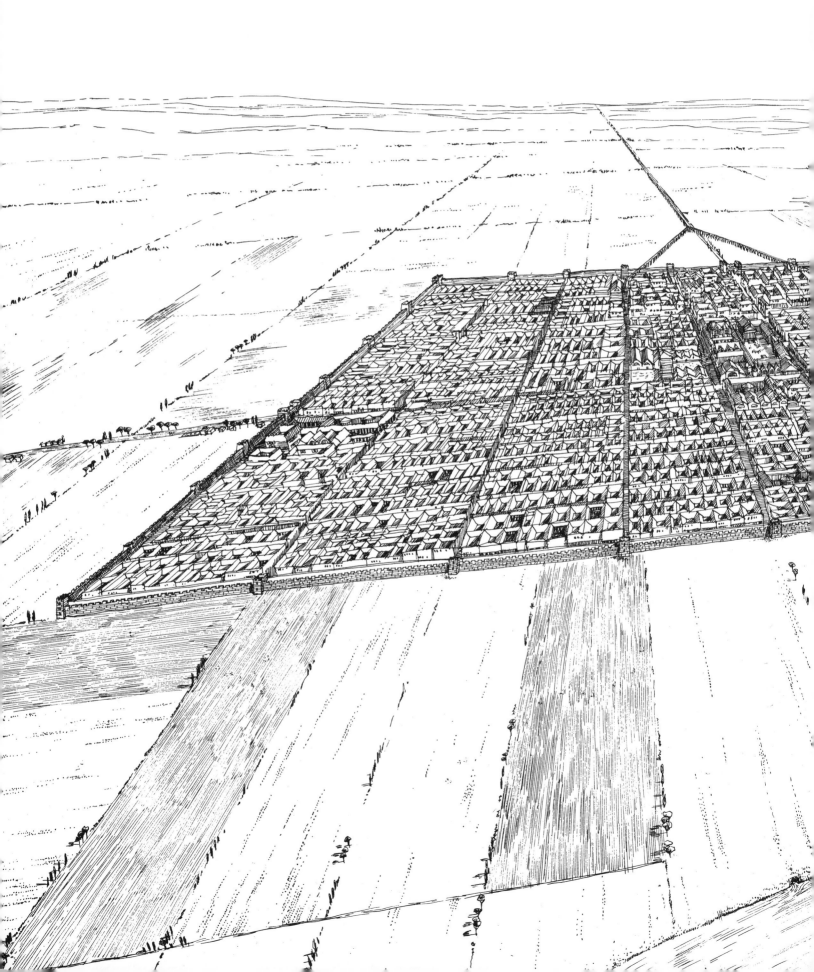

out ideas. The first was the street plan, which maintained order throughout, and the second was the setting aside of land for recreation and entertainment.

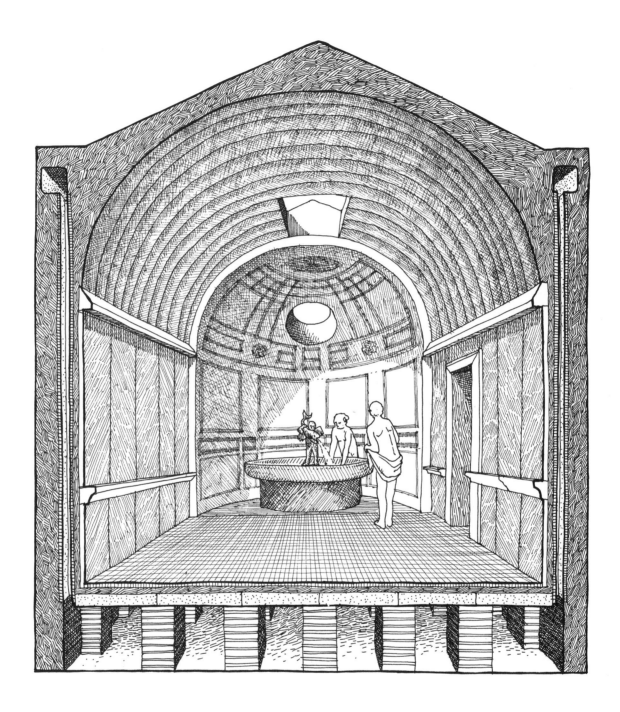

The public baths, called thermae, were not only for washing but also provided a place to meet, talk, exercise, gamble, and even read. Bathing was traditionally accomplished in three stages. First the Romans washed in hot water from a pool in the steamy caldarium. Then they relaxed in a warm-water pool in the tepidarium and finally ended the process with a dive into the cold-water pool of the frigidarium.

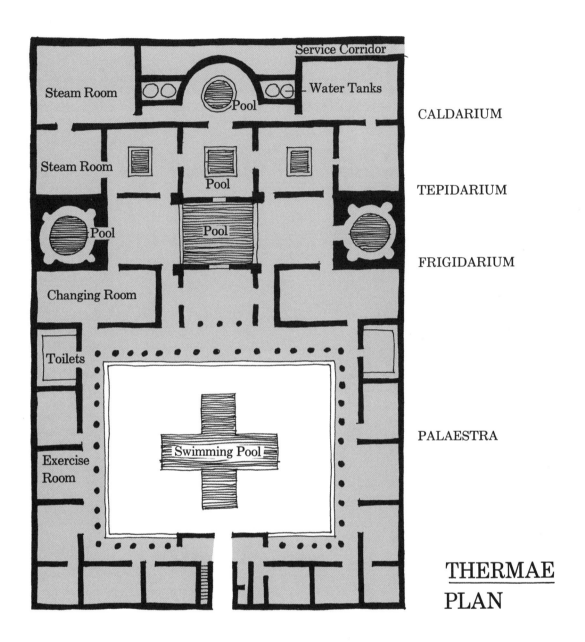

Steam Room

Water Tanks

Service Corridor

Pool

CALDARIUM

Steam Room

Pool

TEPIDARIUM

Pool

Pool

FRIGIDARIUM

Changing Room

Toilets

PALAESTRA

Swimming Pool

Exercise
Room

THERMAE
PLAN

Several small thermae were built during the reign of Augustus, but by A.D. 42 the population had reached 30,000 and the existing facilities were inadequate. The new Emperor Claudius ordered that a much larger thermae be built near the forum on the site of the original baths. A professional demolition company was hired and the old structure, along with a few apartment buildings, was torn down.

THE NEW THERMAE · SECTION

Coffers

Flue

Water Tank

Service Corridor

Water

Furnace

Hypocaust

CALDARIUM

TEPIDARIUM

The mosaic-covered stone floors of the caldarium, tepidarium, and steam rooms were supported two feet off the ground by brick piers, creating a space below the floor called a hypocaust. Hot gases from a furnace outside the building were piped into the hypocaust to heat the rooms. When the hypocaust was

FRIGIDARIUM

Drain to Cloaca

PALAESTRA

full, the gas went up flues — clay pipes in the walls — heating the walls, and out through vents in the vaults.

Suspended over the furnace were large bronze tanks in which water was heated for the baths. The hot water ran into the pool of the caldarium and the overflow, cooling as it went, was piped into the pool of the tepidarium.

The caldarium, tepidarium, changing rooms, steam rooms, exercise rooms, snack bars, and toilets all had tunnel-vaulted ceilings. The larger area of the frigidarium was covered by a series of groin vaults which are created when two tunnel vaults cross each other at a right angle. Each of the cold-water pools in the frigidarium was covered by a dome ceiling with a round opening in the top, called an oculus, to let light in.

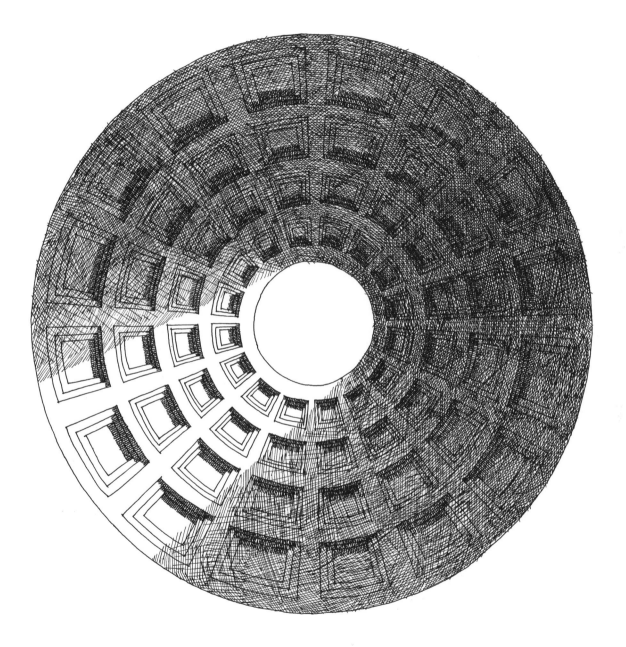

During the construction of both the domes and the vaults, wooden shapes called coffers were fastened on top of the forms. When the concrete had set, the form and coffers were lowered, leaving indentations in the surface of the ceiling which lightened but did not weaken it. This allowed the supporting walls or piers to be somewhat thinner.

Next to the thermae, a grassed area containing a swimming pool was enclosed by a two-story colonnade. This area was called the palestra and was used for exercising and wrestling, among other things. Behind the second floor colonnade and over the entrance a library was built with a collection of scrolls for those who wished to read.

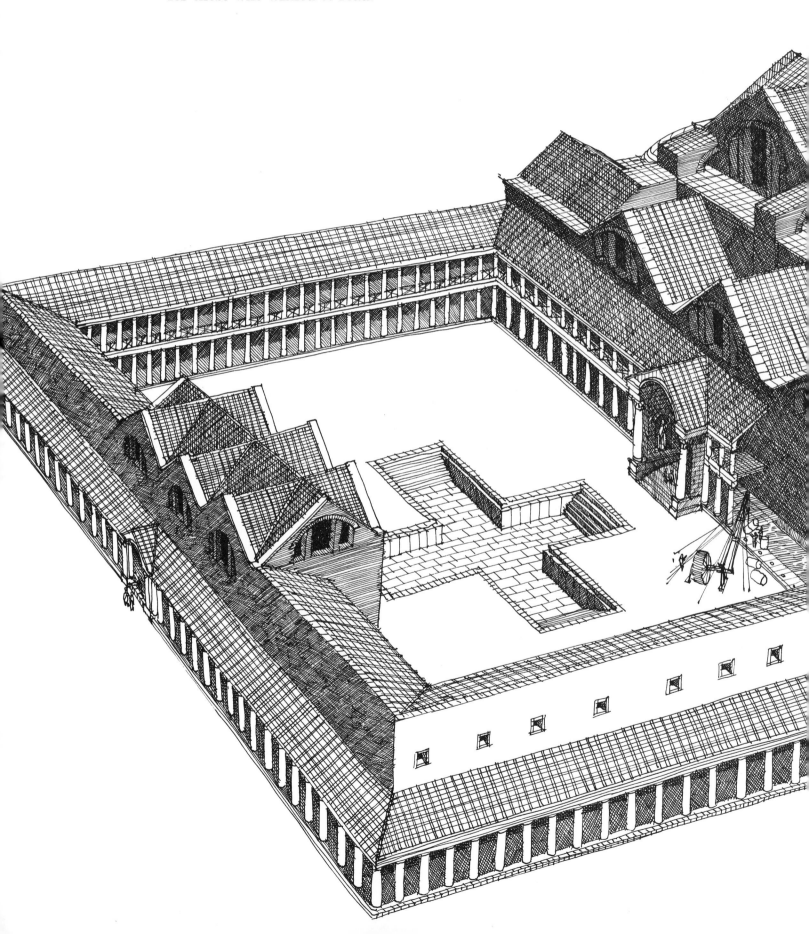

To supply the increased amount of water needed for the larger baths and growing population a second aqueduct was constructed directly on top of the first.

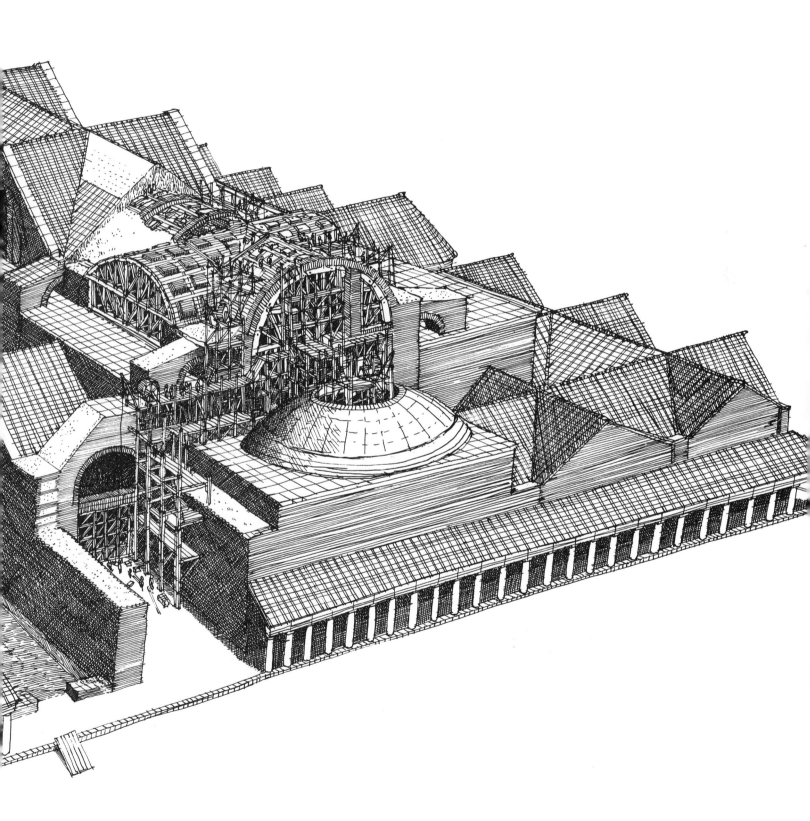

SEATING

POOL

ARENA

THE AMPHITHEATER · PLAN

The last public area to be fully developed was the city's entertainment center. In A.D. 44 the senate voted to build a more permanent amphitheater and theater. Until that time a sloped earth mound lined with stone seats and reinforced by a ring of arches had enclosed both the arena and the stage of the theater.

The original oval shape of the amphitheater was maintained and enlarged. The stone seats now rested on two layers of tunnel-vaulted passages radiating out from the center. These passages were connected by other passages which ran around the arena.

1

2

3

4

CONSTRUCTION OF
THE AMPHITHEATER

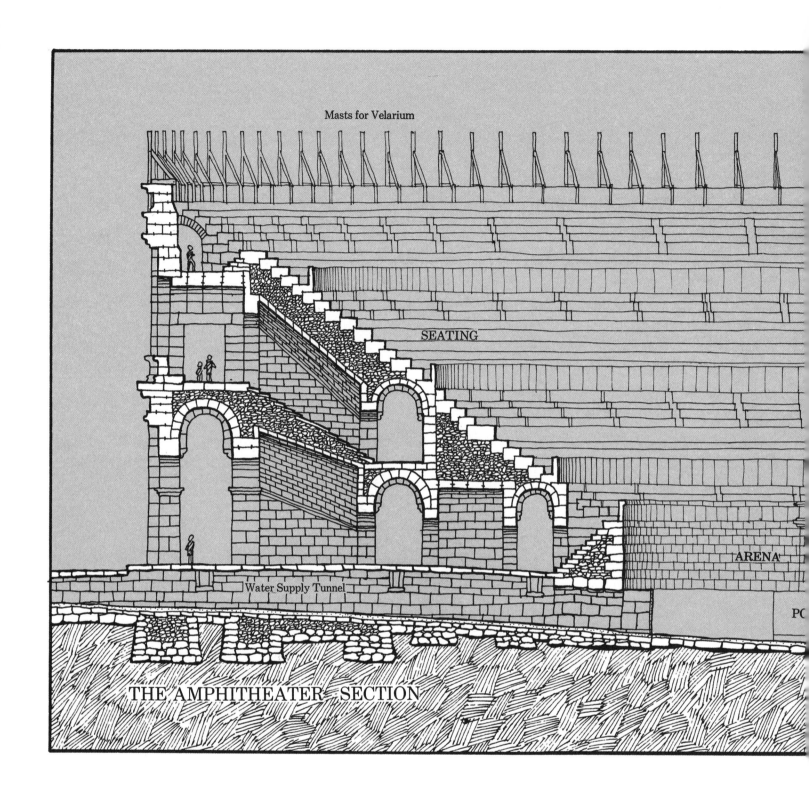

Masts for Velarium

SEATING

ARENA

Water Supply Tunnel

PC

THE AMPHITHEATER SECTION

The arena was sunk several feet into the ground and surrounded by a high wall. Deep pools were built in the floor which could be filled for staging naval battles. When they weren't needed, they were covered by wooden boards and emptied through a canal into the cloaca.

Besides toilets and a snack bar the passages contained ramps and stairways

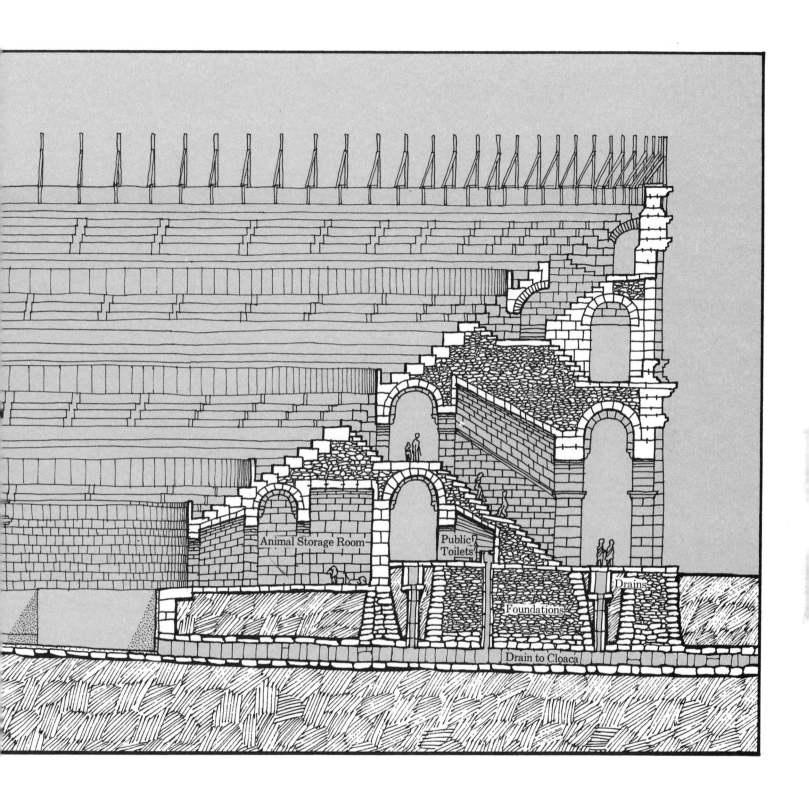

which enabled the entire twenty thousand spectators to enter or leave the structure in less than ten minutes. Wild animals and equipment used in the performances were kept under the lowest seats in rooms which opened onto the arena. The most popular performances involved the deaths of either animals, slaves, or gladiators — men paid to fight each other.

Two rows of arches, one on top of the other, formed the exterior wall of the amphitheater. This wall was constructed of carefully cut stones clamped together with iron and bronze pins. The passages and vaulting were all constructed of stone and concrete. A rope net was suspended above the entire

seating area from wooden masts. If the sun was too hot a canvas roof called a valarium was drawn over the seating area. When it rained during a performance everyone took shelter in the passages.

During the construction of the amphitheater some formwork was accidentally moved before the concrete in the vault had completely set, killing twenty-five slaves, their foreman, and a senator observing the work from the ground. The bodies of the slaves were taken on two carts to a field four miles outside the city and buried in a large pit. The bodies of the senator and foreman were cremated and the ashes sealed in urns. The senator's urn was placed in his elaborate family tomb, much closer to the city but still outside the walls as required by law. The foreman's urn was buried in a public but still respectable graveyard, where his family erected a tombstone in his memory.

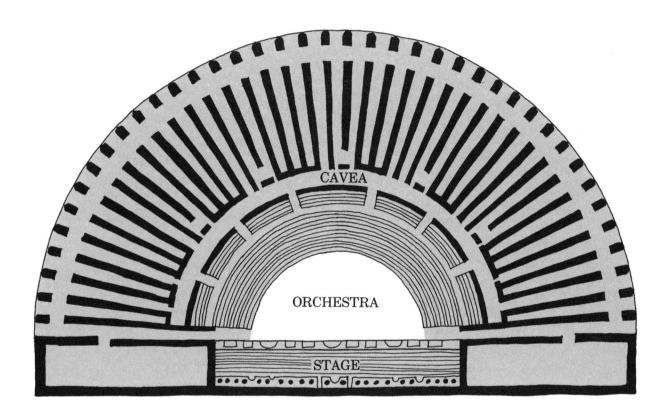

CAVEA

ORCHESTRA

STAGE

THE THEATER · PLAN

Because the senator had always enjoyed plays, his family donated a large sum of money toward the construction of the new theater. The seats were built around a steep semicircular pit called a cavea. Like the seats of the amphitheater they were supported by a network of concrete tunnels. A long wooden stage was constructed across the diameter of the cavea. At both sides of the stage rooms were built for changing and storing costumes.

A curtain could be raised from under the stage for scenery changes. Behind the stage the wall called the frons scaenae was covered with marble columns and architectural ornamentation. This wall reached the same height as the colonnade that was built around the last row of seats in the cavea. Sometimes the actors

performed in the orchestra — the flat semicircular area directly in front of the stage. The most important people sat either on wide seats around the orchestra or in balconies over the side entrances. The theater, too, could be covered by a valarium.

By A.D. 75 both the amphitheater and theater were finished and a festival which lasted twenty-five days was held to celebrate the occasion.

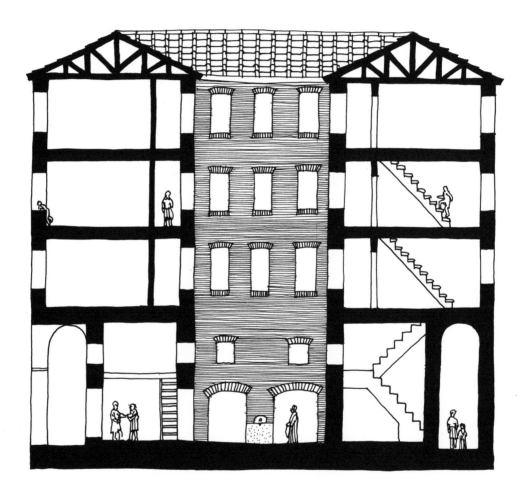

As Verbonia's population steadily climbed, most landlords replaced their small apartment buildings with large apartment blocks. Some, as high as five stories, contained twenty families. To take advantage of this height, which could still be no more than twice the width of the street, the senate passed a law limiting the first apartment blocks to insulae along the northern and western sides of the city. In the winter these buildings would shield the city from the cold wind that blew down the valley.

As in earlier buildings, the apartments in each block were built around a light shaft. The lowest level of the buildings was a series of tunnel-vaulted rooms built side by side and opening onto the sidewalk. These spaces were rented by shopkeepers who constructed a wooden platform on which to live eight feet above the floor. Stables and storerooms around the central courtyard were also rented out.

By A.D. 100 Verbonia's population was almost fifty thousand. Many of the insulae now contained up to eight large apartment blocks and only the wealthiest residents of the city could afford privately owned houses. As the demand increased, old thermae, markets, and temples were torn down and replaced by larger, more adequate structures. The two aqueducts still satisfied the city's

water needs and the one-hundred-and-twenty-year-old sewer system was still operating flawlessly. Because of the efficient organization of farmland and the large number of markets and bakeries, food continued to remain in good supply. The streets, although busy, were not overcrowded. They were still safe and comfortable outdoor areas as originally intended in the master plan.

One hundred and twenty-five years after its founding, Verbonia had reached its limit. With the empire stronger than ever the walls once constructed to keep the enemy out were now serving a more important function — that of keeping the city in.

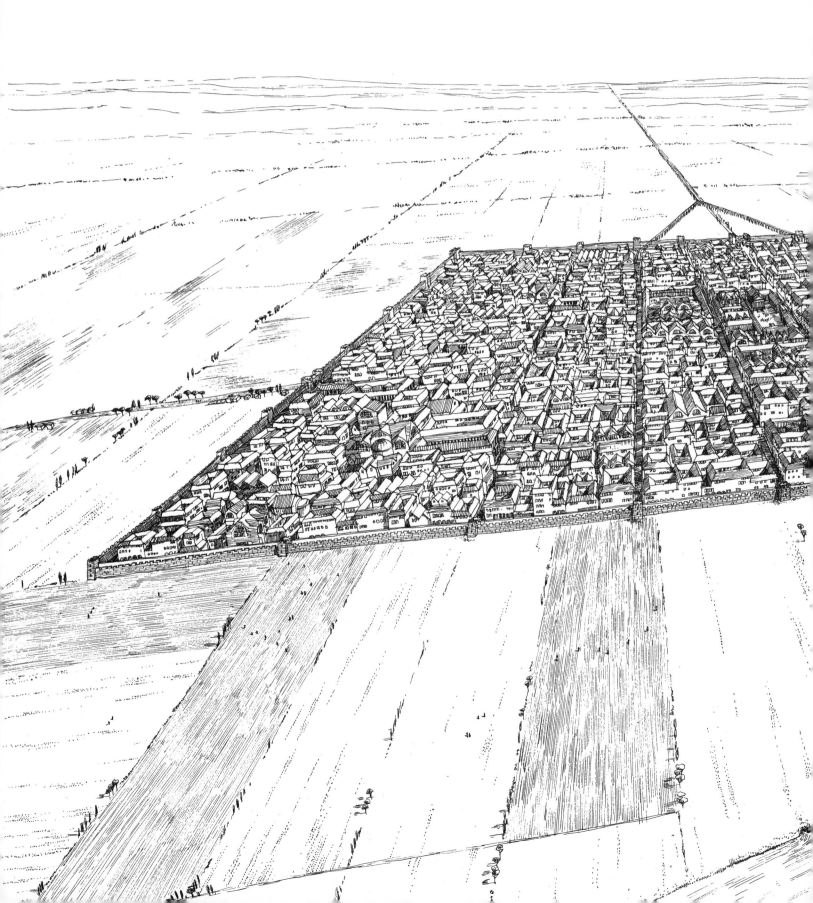

GLOSSARY

AMPHITHEATER
An oval arena completely surrounded by gradually rising rows of seats.

ATRIUM
The largest interior space in a Roman house. It is completely covered by a roof except for the central section which is left open to the sky.

AQUEDUCT
A pipeline specifically built to carry water.

AXLE
The shaft on which a wheel revolves.

CALDARIUM
The heated area of the thermae containing hot water pools.

CARDO
The main north-south road through a Roman city.

CASTRUM
A Roman military camp usually square or rectangular in shape.

CAVEA
The steep semicircular seating area of the theater.

CENTERING
A temporary wooden arch over which a brick or stone arch is constructed. When the mortar sets between the bricks or stones of the permanent arch, the centering is removed.

CHOROBATE
A long wooden surveying instrument used for general siting as well as determining the profile of the land.

CLOACA
A large underground sewer in the form of a tunnel.

COFFERDAM
A water tight enclosure constructed in a river or lake. The water is pumped out of the cofferdam enabling laborers to work directly on the river or lake bed.

COFFERS
Recessed areas in a concrete vault or dome which reduce the weight of the roof.

COLONNADE
A row of columns supporting a horizontal beam or a roof.

COMPLUVIUM
The opening in the roof of the atrium.

CONCRETE
An extremely strong building material made by combining stones of varying sizes and mortar.

CRENELATIONS
The alternating high and low sections of stonework along the top of a defensive wall. The defender is protected behind the high sections while firing his weapon over the lower sections.

DECUMANUS
The main east-west road through a Roman city.

FORGE
A workshop in which metal is heated in a furnace and hammered into shapes for tools and instruments.

FORUM
The government and religious center of a Roman city consisting of an open meeting area surrounded by buildings and colonnades.

FRIGIDARIUM
The area of the thermae containing cold water pools.

GROIN VAULT
The vault created by the intersection of two tunnel vaults at right angles to each other.

GROMA
A surveying instrument consisting of a pole and a horizontal cross from which hang four weighted strings. When the strings hang parallel to the pole the instrument is known to be perfectly vertical and the roads and walls could then be accurately laid out on the ground by siting along the arms of the cross.

HYPOCAUST
The chamber under a raised floor into which hot gases were piped in order to heat the floor.

IMPLUVIUM
The pool in the floor of the atrium which collected the water that fell through the compluvium.

INSULA
A Roman city block, usually square or rectangular in shape.

KEYSTONE
The central locking stone at the top of an arch.

MORTAR
A mixture of sand, lime and water used to cement stones and bricks together. When it dries it becomes very hard.

OCULUS
A round opening or window.

PERISTYLE
The open courtyard or garden in a Roman house surrounded by a colonnade.

PIERS
A free-standing brick, stone or concrete structure similar to a column but usually thicker, used to support an arch.

PILE
A tree trunk stripped of bark and pointed at one end that is then driven into a river bed or marshy area in the construction of a cofferdam or is used to create a sturdy base for a pier.

POMERIUM
The open strip of land along the inner face of the wall around a Roman city. It served as the sacred boundary within which the land was thought to be protected by the gods.

PORTCULLIS
A metal-clad timber grill which could be lowered to seal off the gates of the city.

POZZOLANA
A gravelly substance mixed with regular mortar, enabling it to harden under water.

PROFILE MAP
A drawing which outlines the surface of the land showing the height and depth of hills and valleys.

ROSTRUM
A raised platform from which speeches are delivered.

STUCCO
Heavy plaster.

TEPIDARIUM
The heated area of the thermae containing hot water pools.

THERMAE
Roman public baths.

TRUSS
A wooden frame used to bridge a space too wide to be bridged by a single beam.

TUNNEL VAULT
A continuous semicircular ceiling or roof.

VALARIUM
A canvas roof drawn over a theater or amphitheater to protect the spectators from the sun.